A GLOSSARY OF JUDGES'

DRESSAGE TERMS

LÉONIE M. MARSHALL

J. A. ALLEN

LONDON & NEW YORK

British Library Cataloguing in Publication Data

Marshall, Léonie Mary
    Glossary of judges' dressage terms.
    1. Dressage — Judging — Terminology
    I. Title
    798'.24   SF309.5

    ISBN 0-85131-317-5

Published in Great Britain in 1979 by
J. A. Allen & Company Limited,
1, Lower Grosvenor Place, Buckingham Palace Road,
London, SW1W 0EL
and in the United States of America by
Sporting Book Center, Inc.,
Canaan, N.Y. 12029.
Reprinted 1981
Reprinted 1982
Typeset by Photoprint, Paignton, Devon.
Printed and bound by The Devonshire Press, Torquay, Devon.

ABOVE THE BIT

This is an evasion of the bit.

It is recognised by the fact that the horse carries his head too high and cannot be easily controlled.

Because the head is in the air with the nose well in front of the vertical the action of the bit is ineffective.

The horse will be unbalanced. He will have a hollow back which will make it impossible for him to carry himself and his rider, except with extreme difficulty.

This evasion is a serious fault as it prevents the correct development of the muscles which will hinder the horse's progress. Until it is corrected, training cannot proceed.

Correction

A horse which is above the bit has not been taught, or not understood, that when the rider takes a contact on his mouth, he must yield, not resist.

How does the horse learn to accept the bit?

The answer to this is probably one of the most difficult things to explain, as so much depends on the knowledge, feel and hands of the rider.

Theoretically, the rider closes his legs and feels the mouth, evenly, with both hands until the horse bends at the poll, relaxes his lower jaw and 'gives' to the hand. The rider then must instantly ease the pressure, but not so much as to lose what he has just achieved.

In practice, the procedure can be quite difficult unless the rider is sensitive and knows what he is doing.

Much depends also on the type of mouth the horse has, unmade, made, or spoilt.

In the case of the made mouth, the matter is relatively simple. The rider will close the legs and take up contact. The horse feeling this will bring his head into position with no resistance, and away they can go.

The unmade mouth causes a good deal of confusion amongst riders. Most riders are very much aware that any

1

careless handling of their horse's mouth will cause callouses and in consequence, hardening. Therefore there is a great reluctance on the part of many riders to take much contact at all on the unmade mouth. Oddly enough although their motives are honourable, the result is not what they expect. Little or no contact, will never teach the horse to accept the bit. Only by a firm or 'asking' hand, then easing and lightening of the contact, when the horse has 'given' to the bit, will make him understand.

Many riders are insufficiently interested to make or improve a mouth. Hence, there are many horses who have never been taught to accept the bit and have spoilt mouths.

These horses are a menace, they are resistant to the hands and often turn 'nappy' when someone tries to insist on them doing something which they do not want to do.

With the lack of acceptance incorrect habits occur and many horses get a bad name, unfairly.

With knowledge and understanding these horses can be corrected, but any re-training must necessarily take quite a long time, as the horse must un-learn before he can re-learn. (If nappiness has become confirmed the horse may never be completely corrected, although with patience and determination the situation can be improved).

When there is a lot of resistance as in the case of the spoilt mouth, the rider must basically apply the usual aids, taking a much firmer contact, slightly more leg and overcome the resistance until some relaxation occurs.

In the case of the horse being above the bit, he must be treated as having a spoilt mouth.

The horse should be kept at a slow speed at first, preferably in walk, so that there is no extra impulsion to cope with. Maintaining a slow walk with a firm contact, the rider must make sure that the horse is going forwards. He must not keep a 'dead' pull on the reins, but must move the bit gently in the horse's mouth by squeezing one rein and then the other. As long as the reins are not loosened, after a period of time the horse will lower his head to a better position, the rider should then control this improved head position with a light contact. Most riders give up before this is achieved and the correction is never established. If the rider perseveres and the horse lowers his head, he should be rewarded with a pat on the neck.

Until the horse will accept the bit in walk, the trot should not be attempted.

All this may take several days as it should only be carried out for short periods each day (as long as it takes to achieve a result), but with patience the horse will ultimately learn to keep his head in the correct position.

ABRUPT TRANSITION

A transition is a change from one pace to another, walk to trot, trot to canter etc. or, an alteration of stride within a pace. For example, collection to extension etc.

An abrupt transition usually occurs if the rider has given his aids too suddenly and without sufficient preparation. As a result, balance, rhythm, head-carriage etc. may be lost.

Correction

Throughout the training the rider should aim to make all transitions as smooth as possible.

To achieve this, there are several factors the rider must take into consideration.

First, the rider must allow for the time lapse, however small, which occurs when his thoughts have to be transferred to his muscle system, and in turn, to the horse's brain and muscle system.

Secondly, the rider must prepare the horse and warn him that something is going to happen.

These 'warning' aids are called half halts.

As the half halt is used so much in training, I have taken

this quote from the B.H.S. Rules on dressage, so that the definition is accurate.

The Half Halt

The half halt is a hardly visible almost simultaneous, co-ordinated action of the seat, the legs and the hand of the rider with the object of increasing the attention and balance of the horse before the execution of several movements or transitions to lesser and higher paces. In shifting slightly more weight onto the horse's quarters, the engagement of the hind legs and the balance on the haunches are facilitated, for the benefit of the lightness of the forehand and the horse's balance as a whole.

The half halts correctly used are of vital value in the training of the horse. In the early stages with the young horse the experienced rider uses the half halt in a very minor degree. It may be necessary to use them frequently to help the horse stay in balance and to improve the quality of the steps by making the rhythm constant.

Later, the hind legs may be brought more under the horse by slightly stronger aids, but only when the horse is physically ready to carry more weight on the hindquarters.

If the horse is correctly prepared for the transitions by the use of the half halts to maintain balance, and if there is no resistance to the hand, the rider should be able to take the horse smoothly from one pace to the other. Straightness must also be a vital factor.

ANTICIPATED OR ANTICIPATION

This occurs when the horse thinks he is aware of what is about to happen.

In the case of a transition the horse may try, or succeed in trying, to make the transition before the rider's aid.

Correction

As it is a necessary part of the test for the horse to be

obedient, he must learn to wait for the rider's aids. In training the rider must be careful that he is always in control of what is happening. The horse may not choose what he wants to do nor when, he must wait until he has a directive from his rider.

Some riders find it difficult to concentrate on the way their horses are going but they must choose whether they want an obedient horse or not. It is not fair on the horse to let him choose the pace sometimes and then expect him to be obedient to the rider in a test.

It may sound rather boring to have to teach the horse to be completely controlled but once the horse will wait for the aids he is a much easier and nicer ride.

BACK NOT ROUND
This expression is intended to indicate that the horse is not using his back correctly and instead of swinging upwards towards the rider, he 'holds' his back away, either flat or hollow.

Correction
If the horse is to be a comfortable ride and if he is to progress in his work he needs to be relaxed and supple in the back.

The rider must be very aware when he is riding that he is not coming down heavily in the saddle which will cause discomfort and eventual 'hardening' of the back muscles.

The only way that the horse's back will be nice to 'sit on', is if he is worked with his head and neck in a natural position without resistance and with his hind legs working actively under him. The rider must beware of the horse coming 'above the bit', or too high in his headcarriage, which will cause hollowing of the back. This also prevents the hind legs doing their job effectively.

It is unnecessary to allow the horse to put his head very low in order to get the back round, but the horse should offer to 'lower' if the rein is given. If he does not, it is doubtful if he is using his back correctly.

If the horse does not offer to lower when the rein is given, the rider may not have a good enough acceptance of the bit (see page 7). He should check on this aspect and also try changing pace several times, as this will make the horse 'use' himself more. If he is working harder, he will be more likely to want to stretch his head and neck, which will in turn slightly stretch the back muscles.

BALANCE NOT MAINTAINED

This comment describes the state of the horse when he is either momentarily off balance, or if the balance is generally lacking.

Momentary loss of balance is not necessarily a great crime so long as the horse was balanced in the first place, but if the balance is lost for any length of time many things can go wrong. The horse will probably alter rhythm, be irregular in the stride, come off the bit, fall on the forehand, etc. All these problems will lose the rider many marks.

Correction

Throughout the training of the horse, the rider must work for the perfection of the balance.

The first aim should be to try to put even weight, of the rider and horse, over the horse's four legs, so that no one pair of legs are being overworked.

As the horse is naturally heavy in front due to his head and neck, he may carry too much weight on the forehand.

As he develops physically and strengthens, he must be asked to use his hindquarters more under his body so that they eventually take more of his weight. The forehand will be lightened as a result.

It will be necessary to use steadying aids, constantly, to correct or assist the balance. These are generally called half halts (see page 4) and may be used in varying degrees.

With the young horse the amount of these half halts is merely a slight slowing of the speed, with the rider making sure that the hindlegs still work and do not become inactive.

As the rider will want to maintain light leg aids he may use the schooling whip to assist him.

When using the schooling whip the hand should be kept on the rein, so as not to disturb the contact with the mouth.

As the training progresses, the degree of the half halt may be increased to transfer more weight to the hind-quarters.

BEHIND THE BIT

This is an evasion, with the horse not accepting the bit.

The horse draws back from the bit and will not allow a contact to be taken. The nose is usually behind the vertical which is incorrect.

Correction

The rider should first check that the bits or bit fit correctly and that his horse's teeth are not catching on the bit and causing discomfort. He must check also that he is maintaining a satisfactory contact and that he has not caused the horse to come behind the bit by being heavy handed.

If it is not any of these things the rider should take an even contact with the horse's mouth and give him the feel of the hands. Then he should ask the horse to go forward first at a steady speed, but then increasing the activity to give the pace more impulsion. At the same time he should try to encourage the horse to bring his nose in front of the vertical by allowing his hands any forward movement asked for by the horse.

7

Also vary the pace from a shorter stride to a longer one until there is sufficient energy going into the hand. When altering the pace, do not change 'speed' but try to lengthen or shorten the stride in the same rhythm.

BEHIND THE MOVEMENT
This comment refers to the rider and means that the body of the rider is behind the vertical and he may be putting too much weight on the loins of the horse thus impeding the action of the hind legs and movement of the horse's back.

Correction
When training the horse much concentration is exerted on the way the horse is going, but the rider must constantly check his position as only the correct position will have the right influence on the way the horse is going.

BROKE
This expression is used when the horse changes of his own will, the pace he is in to another. In other words if he is in canter and falls for a moment to trot and then back to canter, that is a 'break' in the pace.

Correction
In training one of the most vital factors is the correct balance of the horse at all times. The rider must be very aware of this point and constantly try to ensure that he assists the horse as much as possible.

Breaks in the pace are usually caused by a loss of balance or possibly a mistaken aid. The rider must make sure the *speed* at which he is riding is not unbalancing the horse. Very often less experienced riders allow their horses to go too fast so that the horse cannot control his own weight, lack of balance must follow.

When the horse is properly balanced he can 'carry

himself', at any pace without falling out of it, with only light contact from the rider's hands and legs.

Half halts (see page 4) play a big part in balancing the paces. The rider should also make sure that his aids are always clear so that the horse will not misunderstand and break the pace for this reason.

CANTER BROKEN

This remark I think, should mean that the pace of three time is not entirely true, but sometimes the comment may refer to a horse cantering croup high, which does give the impression of the horse cantering in two pieces, first the forehand and then the hindquarters.

Correction

I believe the rider should first check that the pace is truly in three time and that the balance (see page 6) is correct.

Then concentrate on the hindquarters and try to work the horse to improve the length of the stride. This means using the half halts and constantly correcting the rhythm and balance. Also the canter may need to be more forward with a better movement of suspension between the strides. Variation in the pace, i.e. coming from working canter to a degree of collection and back to working, can help to improve the suspension.

CHANGING RHYTHM

This comment refers to an alteration of the steps within a pace.

Instead of moving with regular, steady strides, the horse for one reason or another breaks the length of the stride for one or more steps. This alters the rhythm.

Correction

First of all check on the speed of the pace, and make

sure that in no way is the horse unbalanced. Secondly, make certain that the horse is accepting the bit evenly on both sides of his mouth, by testing him with the hand. Squeeze a little first on one side and then on the other to make sure that the 'yield' is equal.

The rider must then concentrate on the rhythm he wants and if it helps, count the footfalls.

In walk, the footfalls should be in four time, each foot coming to the ground separately.

In trot, the rhythm is two time, as the legs come to the ground diagonally. For example, the near fore and off hind, and then the off fore and near hind.

The canter is three time, for example, leading with the near fore, the horse will start with the off hind followed by the near hind and off fore, and then the near fore, followed by a moment of suspension.

CIRCLE TOO LARGE/SMALL/SQUARE

Often as a judge one has to deduct marks for incorrect size and shape of circles. This is rather a waste of marks so it is worth finding out how to ride the right size.

Correction

First, a circle must be round. The rider must try to visualise the circle on the ground and look ahead to see where he is going.

Secondly, it helps some riders to aim at certain points on the circle to help to get them in the right place. On a 20 metre (66 feet) circle the rider should aim for the four points, as shown.

Having achieved the correct size circle, the rider must curve the horse to the shape of the circle and keep the bend constant.

He should hold the horse to the circle with the outside rein, using the inside leg to keep the horse out and bent slightly. The inside rein may be used a little against the

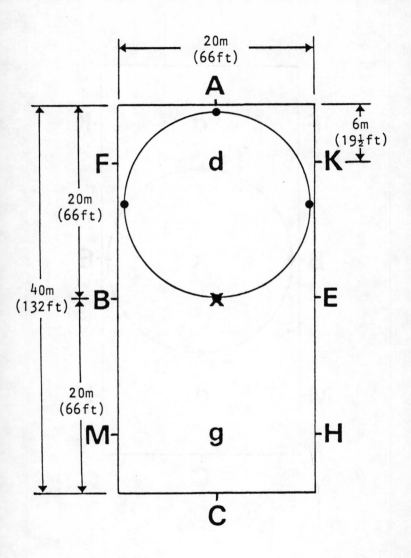

Fig 1   Arena & 20 metres diameter circle

11

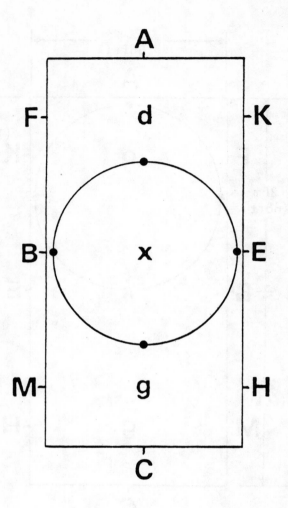

Fig 2   Circle — 20 metres diameter

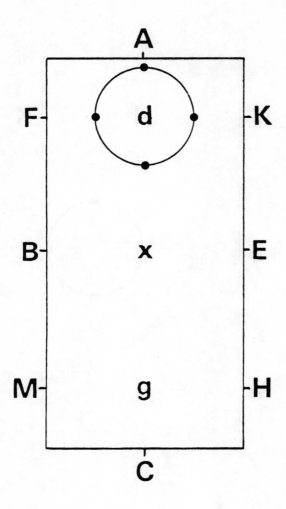

Fig 3   Circle — 10 metres diameter

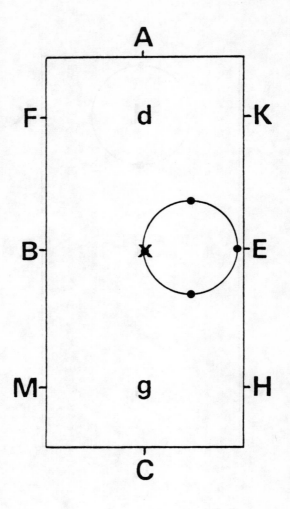

Fig 4   Circle — 10 metres diameter

14

neck to work in conjunction with the outside rein and also create some flexion.

The outside leg must control the hind quarters and prevent them flying out.

The speed and rhythm of the pace must be steady and regular.

CROUP HIGH

This can be seen most easily in the canter, and means that the croup of the horse is going 'up', at each stride. As the quarters should lower and come 'under' the horse more and more during training in order to lighten the forehand, this would be incorrect.

Correction

It is difficult to correct if it becomes established, and is usually caused by stiffness, and/or being on the forehand.

If the balance is correct and the horse accepting the bit with a round back, the rider must aim to increase the activity of the hind legs, encouraging them to come under the body by using variation of pace. For comments on balance, see page 6.

When the hindlegs come under the body, the croup will have to lower and the horse's weight will be carried by the quarters and not by the forehand.

CROOKED HALT

This means that the horse has stopped with his quarters to one side or the other of his forehand so that he is not straight.

Correction

A crooked halt is often caused by resistance to the hand so make sure the horse is accepting the bit (see page 1).

Too much impulsion sometimes causes crookedness, as the horse cannot cope with himself if he is going too fast.

The horse may not be accepting the control of the rider's legs in the approach to the halt. He must allow the rider to 'hold' the quarters.

The rider should also be able to control the shoulders of the horse and not allow the horse to put more weight onto one shoulder than the other.

If the horse does halt crooked, the rider should not attempt to correct it by using one leg and then the other, this will only cause more crookedness.

He may try to go forward a couple of strides to straighten the horse, or he may try to move the forehand a little to get it in line with the quarters, but this is more difficult, and the horse and rider need to understand the shoulder in exercise (see page 45).

CUTTING CORNERS

This refers to the degree, that the rider takes or does not take, when riding his horse into the corners of the arena. There is much confusion over this, from the rider who goes straight into the corner and turns sharply to get out, to those who waste a lot of the arena by not going anywhere near the corner, as in this case.

Correction

With this problem, riders must bear in mind the stage of training of their horse.

Obviously the more supple and trained the horse the deeper the rider can go into the corner.

In early stages when the horse is not yet collected, it is a mistake to go too deep and risk upsetting the pace and balance of the horse.

A rough guide to the riding of a corner is as follows:-

Take two points on either side of the corner and ride a true curve between them with the horse bent in the direction he is going. A wrong bend in the corners or no bend at all is incorrect.

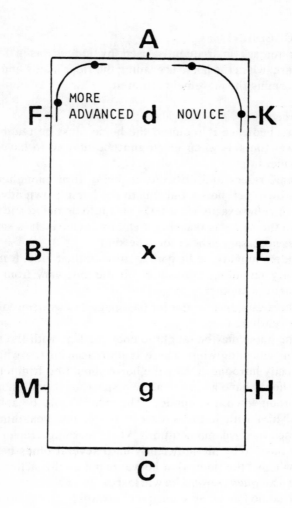

Fig 5 Riding corners correctly

DISOBEDIENT

This remark is frequently used by judges, as a short remark, when the horse is evading the rider's aids and not performing the movement required.

Correction

As obedience is required the horse must be taught to answer the aids when given and not allowed to have his own ideas.

Some riders find difficulty in being firm enough with their own 'pet' horse, but it is to the horse's own advantage to know exactly what he is meant to be doing and it is much the same as teaching a child to behave. It is sometimes necessary to be cruel to be kind!

Riders must try to be consistent with their aids. It must be very muddling to the horse if the aids vary from one moment to another.

The acceptance of the bit (see page 1) has been talked about earlier.

The horse may be taught to obey the legs with the help of the schooling whip. There is no reason, if the whip is correctly introduced, why the horse should be frightened. He should have a very healthy respect for it and jump to attention when it is applied. The rider should be able to 'tap' him with it to increase activity, not beat him to extract forward momentum! When learning, the horse may have to be hit sufficiently hard several times before he will give the rider what he wants but by this action and the *subsequent reward* he will learn.

What do I mean by subsequent reward?

All that is necessary to teach the horse that he has complied correctly to the aids is a pat on the neck. Titbits are a nuisance. The horse cannot be stopped five times round the school for a lump of sugar, but he can have five pats on the neck and can and does learn very quickly from it.

DISUNITED

This comment refers to the horse in canter when the sequence of the legs becomes, or is incorrect. For left canter the correct sequence is:

Off hind
Near hind and off fore
Near fore.

When the canter is disunited the sequence could be:-

Off hind
Near hind and near fore
Off fore

or

Near hind
Off hind and off fore
Near fore

Quite often the horse will change legs behind on a circle or corner. Sometimes he will change in front only. The situation is generally caused by lack of balance, and/or stiffness in the back.

Correction

The first thing to do is to ensure that the horse is working 'in balance', and that he is also accepting the bit (see page 1), as resistance in the mouth will hinder any corrections.

The next important factor is the control of the hind-quarters. The horse must be taught to 'listen' to the rider's outside leg which should control any outward swing of the quarters. If the hindlegs do not follow the forelegs it will be easy for the horse to change behind, particularly on a circle when he is asked for 'bend'. The rider must be careful when asking for flexion to the inside that he is not using more rein than leg, and that he is controlling the outside of the horse as much as the inside. He must maintain an even pressure on both sides of the horse whenever possible. (For comments on balance, see page 6).

DID NOT CHANGE DIAGONAL

Some judges do make this comment about the rider, although marks are not deducted. They mean that in the trot, when a change of rein is made the rider has not changed from diagonal to the other. The horse trots in two time, first, one foreleg and the opposite hind leg come to the ground, then the other foreleg and opposite hindleg. These are called diagonals and in rising trot the rider will rise on one pair of legs and sit when the other pair come to the ground.

Correction

A rider correction. He must learn how to change from one diagonal to the other and know which one he is on without looking to see. It is necessary to do this when changing the rein, in order to show that the horse's muscles are evenly developed on both sides.

There are very many horses which are very uneven and subsequently very stiff on one side because of being ridden on one diagonal only.

When rising at the trot the rider may glance at the outside foreleg or shoulder. When that foreleg comes to the ground and the shoulder comes back, the rider should sit. To change the diagonal the rider must sit for one extra stride and then continue rising.

DOWN IN FRONT

This is really just another way of saying 'on the forehand',

20

except that on the forehand relates to the weight of the horse on the shoulders whereas 'down in front' I think has the additional disadvantage in that the whole front of the horse is too low, not just the shoulders.

Correction

The rider must look to the balance primarily, and by the use of the half halts (see page 4) transfer weight from the forehand to the quarters.

He should also consider the outline or silhouette of the horse, and if the neck and head are below the withers, this must surely mean that the front is too low.

By correcting the balance, the outline should improve, but if it does not improve sufficiently, the rider should seek practical expert help.

EARLY TO WALK/TROT ETC.

A requirement in the tests is to perform the transitions at various markers. This shows the obedience, suppleness and willingness of the horse to comply with his rider's wishes.

In some cases the horse may anticipate or simply change the pace before he is told. This expression is used in this instance.

Correction

The rider should practice transitions at a marker. A guide is that when the rider's leg is on the marker the horse should be doing what he has been asked. This means good 'preparation' by the rider.

A young horse needs plenty of warning of a coming transition.

The rider should use the half halts to help the horse adjust his balance in order to make the transition smooth, straight and at the designated place.

(For comments on half halts, see page 4).

FALLING IN

This applies to the horse when, at any pace, he goes round a corner or circle leaning over to the inside, or putting too much weight on the inside shoulder. Sometimes he will do it momentarily, and sometimes most of the time.

Correction

Riders must be aware that the horse needs to be 'upright' when cornering or circling. This means making sure that the horse's shoulders are taking even weight and that the inside shoulder is not overloaded.

To do this, the bend should be improved, and the response to the rider's inside leg.

If the horse 'lies' on the rider's leg and ignores his aid to create bend or push him out to the circle the rider should use the schooling whip to make the horse 'listen' to the leg, and make sure he is yielding properly to the bit on the inside.

It is probably best to work at walk and achieve a better bend at that pace. Then work up to the other paces. The horse often uses too much impulsion causing him to lean against his rider's leg, so probably he will need slowing down and impulsion temporarily reduced.

FALLING OUT

This may mean that the horse's outside shoulder is escaping on a corner, circle, or in shoulder in, etc, or it may mean that the whole horse is leaving the original line to the outside.

If the comment was, 'Quarters falling out' it would mean that the forehand was in the correct position, but the quarters had left the original line.

Correction

Many riders are not sufficiently aware that the outside of the horse needs just as much, or more, control as the inside. Because so much is talked about 'bend', they concentrate their efforts on the inside rein. However, this frequently causes much more bend in the neck than in the rest of the horse, and this is incorrect, and not a true bend.

If the rider thinks more about the outside rein, both for control and support, he should avoid loosing the outside shoulder. If he also makes quite certain he has not got too much bend in the neck this should help too.

If the whole horse 'falls out' when bend is created, then the rider's outside leg and rein are both at fault.

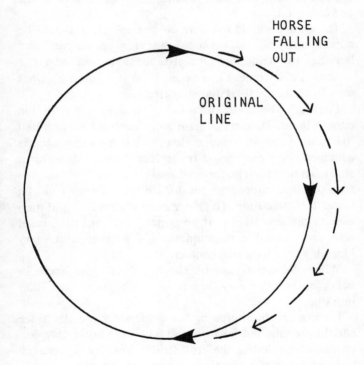

HORSE
FALLING
OUT

ORIGINAL
LINE

Fig 6   Horse falling out

FELL INTO TROT

This describes what happens to the horse, sometimes in the transition from the canter to the trot.

Because the horse's balance in canter is lacking, as the aid to slow up is given, the weight rushes forward and the whole forehand is overloaded at the point when the transition is made.

Correction

The canter pace should be improved. Many riders do not spend sufficient time making their canters rhythmic and balanced.

The canter should not only be one speed, it should be adjustable. The rider should be able to shorten and lengthen the stride without resistance to the hand and leg.

Some improvement can be made to the canter by work on a 20 metre (66 feet) diameter circle.

First get the horse into his normal canter with the correct bend. Then try to gain more control by using half halts (see page 4). When a slower and/or shorter step is achieved the rider should try to 'hold' these steps for a short distance then go forward again.

In the short steps, the tension on the rein must not be same the whole time. The rider must always feel and then ease to make certain that he is not 'carrying' the horse, who must be able to maintain his balance and carry himself with a light rein contact.

When the canter can be shortened with the horse in balance, the rider may then try to work on the transition into trot.

Having got the horse into a balanced state the rider should give the aid for trot, and when the horse 'breaks' immediately control the trot strides and try to balance them also, not allowing the horse to race forward.

The back must be rounded in the transition so the horse's head must not on any account be pulled up, but on the other hand he should not be allowed to 'dive' down either.

It may help the rider to rise in the first few strides of trot, until it is controlled, as this will prevent any inadvertant bumping about which the rider may do if the transition is a little rough, which it may be at first.

When the horse is balanced in the transition, the rider may wish to 'sit' so as to be able to engage the hindquarters properly for the trot.

FLAT CANTER

This remark is usually used when there is insufficient suspension between the canter strides.

Correction

Each three time stride in the canter should be followed by a moment of suspension when the horse is in the air.

Stiffness in the back and the hindquarters not sufficiently under the horse, often cause a flat canter. Improvement can be made by first controlling the speed, this will automatically help the hindlegs to come under the horse. This will also help him to 'carry' himself and instead of merely thrusting him forward, will start to push him 'up' a little as well. Thus the canter begins to have a 'jump' in it and the suspension will improve.

The rider should then concentrate on the rhythm and regularity.

If there is stiffness of the back the rider should employ the shoulder in exercise (see page 45) to improve the horse's suppleness.

FORGING

This is when the toe of the hind shoe catches on the heel of the forefoot and makes a clicking noise. It may only happen occasionally or in some cases quite a lot. It happens mainly in trot.

Correction

It occurs almost entirely due to lack of balance, so this is where to start the improvement.

Sometimes a horse will begin to 'forge' if he is over-tired, so this should be born in mind. (For comments on balance, see page 6).

FOUR TIME

This comment describes the canter when the footfalls are all separate instead of in a sequence of three time.

The correct sequence should be:-

Outside hindleg

Inside hindleg, outside foreleg together

Inside foreleg

Correction

This situation almost always occurs due to lack of impulsion, so this is the first thing to try to correct.

Horses which have 'flat' or 'broken' canters, may also canter in four time. (For comments on impulsion, see page 29).

GRINDING TEETH

This is a most annoying habit and one which loses a mark per movement if it occurs.

Instead of a true acceptance of the bit and hands, the horse will grind his teeth together for various reasons, such as being upset, excited or merely resistant.

Correction

Make certain that the horse is not apprehensive or tense and that he fully understands the aids.

If he is relaxed in his body, then the rider should concentrate very patiently on improving the understanding and acceptance of the aids, using plenty of repetition and reward to improve the horse's confidence in his rider.

If grinding becomes too much of a habit it is almost impossible in some cases to make a correction, so if the horse does start, the rider should really go back in his work and start again, concentrating on the horse's state of mind.

Over excitement often is the cause of the horse starting to grind, or a demonstration of impatience. In this case the rider should keep the impulsion subdued and try to calm the horse.

HEAD UP
A momentary evasion of the horse, coming above the bit.

Often horses put their heads up for a moment when moving into canter.

Correction
The rider must work from the beginning to obtain the acceptance of the bit.

He must work the horse in a co-ordinated way keeping enough impulsion that the horse can go forward without struggling, but not too much which might cause him to lose his balance. If the balance is alright, the head position should be steady and there should be no alteration.

The rider is responsible for the steadiness of the position by the co-ordination of his leg and hand, and the steadiness of his contact. If the contact is loose or intermittent the horse's head is unlikely to be still. (For comments on acceptance of the bit, see page 1).

HOLLOW BACK
Means that the top line of the horse from the nose to the tail is concave as opposed to convex.

Correction
A hollow back is incorrect because the horse's head and hindquarters are in such a position that he cannot perform

in balance, come on the bit, or engage the hindquarters. Therefore it is a disaster!

First correct the mouth, bringing the horse's head to a position where the bit can act properly. If the mouth is put right, everything else should improve.

The horse should be worked at a slow speed to bring the hindquarters underneath him, and the rider should temporarily avoid sitting trot, until the horse is able to use his back instead of holding it stiffly away from the rider. In some cases it may be necessary to work the horse with his head very low, in order to stretch the back muscles, but this does not mean that he should be allowed to go on the forehand.

He should be worked 'in balance', and only then should the rider allow or encourage, the head to lower for a few strides or maybe a few minutes. The horse having had the chance to 'round' his back and stretch and relax the muscles, should then be asked to come up into the correct position and work on. The rider may wish to read further about acceptance of the bit and balance, (see pages 1 and 6).

HURRIED

Usually refers to the paces and means that the horse is rushing along without showing any real rhythm.

It can also mean that a turn such as a pirouette has been hurried, lacking rhythm and control.

Correction

First, slow down, even if it feels as though you have no impulsion. Then really think about creating some regular rhythm in the stride at the various paces.

It may help to count the footfalls, the walk four time, trot two time and canter three time, but riders should try to develop a 'feel' for rhythm coming from an awareness of balance and length of stride.

HALT EARLY OR LATE

This means that the horse has halted before or after the marker.

Correction

There may be various reasons why a halt comes in the wrong place such as resistance to the aids, lack of impulsion etc, but generally it is up to the rider to make it accurate. He should aim to halt when his leg is level with the marker and in the case of halt at 'A', when the horse's body is directly over the centre line. Marks are often lost because this is not complied with.

IMPULSION LACKING

The remark is made if the horse has insufficient energy to keep him going forward at a regular speed, or if he is almost dropping into a lower pace.

Correction

There is a general misunderstanding about impulsion. It is not speed. It is the energy in the hindquarters, which can be built up by the use of exercises, so that the horse is able to propel himself forward without difficulty, and do what his rider wishes. If the hindquarters are not underneath the horse's body, the impulsion will be misplaced and if the hindlegs are working behind the quarters, the horse will be thrusting forward all the time and will not be balanced.

If the hindlegs come well under the horse he will push himself up a little as well as forward, which will give spring to the stride and he will be able to support himself, his weight and that of his rider.

In the early stages of a horse's training too much impulsion should not be expected. If the rider creates a lot of energy in the quarters, the horse will not have the balance to cope with it.

Therefore the impulsion must be sufficient for the horse to work actively in balance, and only gradually as training progresses and the horse develops his physique, may the impulsion be built up.

When horses lack impulsion, it is generally because they have been brought to a slower speed without the rider making sure that the hindlegs remain active.

The schooling whip may be employed to make the hindquarters work more and this means the bending of all the joints, rather than making the horse go faster. A longer stride is not necessarily required.

IMMOBILITY INSUFFICIENT

When a halt is not completely still, this remark may be used. The horse may have altered the head position, or moved a leg, or merely not halted long enough. Sometimes a test will state the length of time for a halt.

Correction

Every well mannered horse should halt and stand still and it is one of the first things for the rider to insist upon.

Some horses, especially thoroughbreds, get rather fidgety, and some even threaten to rear if made to stand. If the horse gets worked up over halts, the rider must try to calm him and get him more relaxed.

Avoid holding on to the reins too tightly at the halt. Make sure the horse is only on a light contact with the hand and leg.

Once he is relaxed, practice plenty of halts from walk and pat him when he does stand still. Try to keep him straight because if he stops in balance he will be more likely to keep still.

INACTIVE

Most judges put this remark when the hind legs of the horse appear lazy, and are not coming under the horse, and the hocks are not bending, but remain rather straight.

Correction

An active hind leg is one which bends at the hock and comes well under the horse's body, so that he can push himself up a little and forward, with maximum effect and minimum effort.

To make a lazy horse active, the rider must use the aid of the schooling whip. Because of its length it can be used lightly on the quarters, without the rider removing his hand from the reins and thus disturbing the contact.

The rider must not drive the horse forward at a fast speed. In fact, the hocks are usually made more active at a fairly slow speed, because they have to work a lot harder.

The whip may have to be used quite a lot to begin with until the lazy horse learns to respect the leg and listen to it, when applied lightly.

A few taps by the whip on a reasonably well schooled horse will increase the energy in the hind quarters and make the hind legs more active.

INATTENTIVE

Means that the horse is not listening to the aids of his rider. His mind is elsewhere and his attention is outside the arena.

Correction

From the beginning the young horse should pay attention to what he is being asked to do and learn to obey the aids.

Young horses must learn to concentrate on what they are being taught and not on what is going on around them.

Some are better than others.

It is a good idea to work a horse in places where there are distractions. Start with one thing at a time, things like other animals, the dog, the cat, cows, sheep etc. Then of

31

course traffic. Cars which rush past on the other side of the hedge.

Horses will be distracted by almost anything. Birds, flapping plastic flags, paper bags, umbrellas, even leaves falling in the hedge!

Although the young horse will be startled to begin with he will gradually know about all these things and as he becomes trained will learn to ignore them, so long as his rider is firm and does not let him look around and as long as his aids are interesting and keep the horse's attention. Some horses are genuinely frightened by distractions and need to be calmed whereas others are just naughty.

INSUFFICIENT IMPULSION See IMPULSION LACKING, page 29.

IRREGULAR
Refers to the stride of the horse when one or more strides are in a different rhythm, or are shorter or longer than the others.

Correction

If the horse is worked at home consistently, in a regular rhythm, and the rider controls the length of the strides, he will learn to carry himself correctly and stay regular at each pace.

Occasionally there may be an alteration, due to a piece of uneven ground, a momentary loss of balance, a mistake made by the rider, such as an involuntary shift of weight, movement of leg, hand etc. This is unfortunate but not a serious mistake, so long as the horse is working normally with good regularity.

If the horse repeatedly gets this comment in a test, the rider must take a serious view of this fault, as consistent irregularity will lose many marks.

The steps may be irregular due to the mouth not being

quite even on both sides or there being an evasion of the bit. Or, the horse may be stiff on one side more than the other and may not be taking equal length steps. This will mean suppling exercises such as 'shoulder in' to make the muscles even and more concentration by the rider to control the steps. For additional comments on acceptance of the bit and shoulder in, see pages 1 and 45.

JUMPED INTO CANTER

Sometimes in transition from trot to canter the horse will literally make a stride as though about to jump something, with the front legs higher off the ground than the hind legs. The head usually goes up too and the neck is raised.

Correction

The horse must be made more obedient to the rider's aid, giving an immediate but smooth reaction to a light aid. Practice on a circle going from canter to trot to canter, demanding an instant answer to each aid. The horse will then become more alert and will be waiting for some directive instead of plodding round mentally asleep. If he should raise his head, neck and forehand, he is not going forward with enough impulsion, the canter-trot-canter exercise should improve this also.

LABOURED

This describes a pace or a movement when it is a tremendous effort for the horse and he can hardly cope with it.

Correction

Improve the activity and impulsion by using the schooling whip and riding transitions to get the hind quarters under the horse.

If he is better balanced and more active he will be able to do what is asked more easily. For additional comments on balance and impulsion, see pages 6 and 29.

LACKING COLLECTION

Means that when collection is asked for the amount shown by horse and rider is insufficient.

Correction

It may be difficult to gauge the amount of collection required, as so many different examples of it are seen.

Some riders go quite slowly with a lot of elevation.

Some ride much more forward.

Some requirements are obvious. The horse must show that he can come together more than at any other pace. His quarters must be lowered slightly and his hind legs come well under him. He must be very active and full of controlled energy. The forehand must be light, with the head and neck raised, the head bent at the poll and lower jaw relaxed showing no resistance.

The horse is compressed into a ball of lightly controlled impulsion.

If any of the above aspects are not seen, the collection may be insufficient.

To achieve true collection requires a tremendous amount of dedicated work on the basic schooling, i.e. straightness, balance, acceptance of the bit, etc. If any of these are lacking the collection will never be really good.

LACKING IMPULSION See IMPULSION LACKING page 29.

LACKING RHYTHM

A pace or movement which lacks rhythm is one which does not have regular even steps.

Correction

A good deal of concentration is required by the rider.

Some horses naturally have a good rhythm and some do not.

34

Even horses who do not can be corrected, if ridden carefully. The rider must aim at a steady controlled speed without too much impulsion to start with, and regular steps with even length.

It may help to count the footfalls in the various paces.

If the horse is not relaxed mentally and physically he will not develop his rhythm, so any tenseness or stiffness must be avoided or overcome. (For comments on footfalls, see pages 9, 19, 26, 50 and 59.

LATE BEHIND

This is a comment made with reference to the flying change. In the moment of suspension in the canter, the horse should make the flying change.

In a true change the fore and hind leg on the same side come forward together, but in the late change, the foreleg may come first followed by the hind leg, a stride or half stride later, and vice versa. Some judges may use the expression 'late change' to mean the same thing.

Late change can also mean late to the rider's aid!

Correction

If the horse persistently changes late behind, it can be very difficult to put right, and it is probably best to put the problem into the hands of an expert. If the rider wishes to attempt the correction himself he should first make sure that the canter itself is alright and the horse is not hollowing his back. The strides must be big and round with a clear moment of suspension.

Work on the simple changes through walk and trot. The horse should be able to change from one leg to the other with only one stride at walk or trot between the canters and must be extremely obedient to the aids. The rider, when he asks for the flying change must ask a fraction before the moment of suspension so that the horse after the period in the air lands on the new leading leg.

LEANING IN. See FALLING IN Page 22.

LEANING ON THE BIT
This is when the horse is relying on the hands of his rider for support. There is too much weight on the forehand and in particular on the bit.

Correction

Using half halts, the rider must improve the balance to reduce the weight on the forehand.

He must then teach the horse to accept the bit so that he will rest on it lightly.

There is nothing more exhausting for the rider than to have the horse leaning and it is quite unnecessary to put up with it, as many riders seem to do. It does require rather a lot of hard work but it is worth the effort! (For additional comments on the acceptance of the bit, half halts and balance, see pages 1, 4 and 6).

LENGTHENING INSUFFICIENT
This could apply to any increase in the length of stride within a pace, i.e. collection to working, working to extension etc. where the horse does not show enough difference between the two changes of pace.

Correction

Most horses find it almost impossible to lengthen correctly before they can shorten the stride. Therefore I think it is necessary to teach the horse to be able to carry himself on a short stride in order to put the hind quarters in a position where they can propel him forward without difficulty.

Once the quarters are 'under' the horse he can be asked to 'push off' and give some length. The degree of length must necessarily depend on the stage of the horse's training. It is a great mistake to make the horse stretch too far before he is ready, as it may cause him to put his hind legs behind him, which impedes true impulsion and is much more of a strain on the loins.

When showing a longer stride the rider must know what is required at the standard he is riding and make sure that he defines the transitions clearly before and after the lengthening.

LOST RHYTHM

This applies to a rhythmic stride which for one reason or another briefly loses the rhythm.

Correction

If there is already a rhythm in the paces, a momentary loss is not all that serious, unless it recurs frequently.

The rider should check on his balance and try to ride with more concentration. (For comments on balance, see page 6).

LOOPS NOT EQUAL

There are various movements involving three or more loops. They should be of equal size and if they are not, marks are lost.

Correction

The rider is obviously responsible for the size and equality of the loops. Often they are not ridden equally because the horse is easier on one rein than the other. The very reason for the exercise is to see that the horse can perform well on both reins and that his muscles are evenly developed. Most horses do find work easier on one side just as people are right or left handed.

Riders should be aware that they themselves . are stronger on one side and weaker on the other and must be careful when schooling not to have the wrong effect on their horses.

Equal amount of work on both reins is important but if the horse is finding the work difficult on one rein, then work him a little more on that side, till corrected.

LOOP ON TWO TRACKS
Some of the movements in the tests require the horse — when cantering — to either return to the track after a half circle on the same leg, or make a loop up the side of the arena which involves a small amount of counter canter. Sometimes on the return to the track, instead of the hind legs following the fore legs, the horse will go sideways in half pass. This defeats the object of the exercise and so will be marked down.

Correction
Try to make sure that the hind legs are following the fore legs, and that the hindquarters are under control.

MOVED AT HALT
This is when the horse has made the halt satisfactorily and then made a movement of the head, or perhaps stepped back, rested a leg, or shifted the quarters slightly.

Correction
The rider must make sure that he can halt and stand still at any given moment and in a variety of circumstances, such as wind, rain, etc.

The horse must know that to move is not allowed and that he will be scolded, but when he stands still he may be given a pat or word of praise.

NECK TOO SHORT
This is a rather ambiguous term, as it sounds as though the judge is criticising the conformation of the horse.

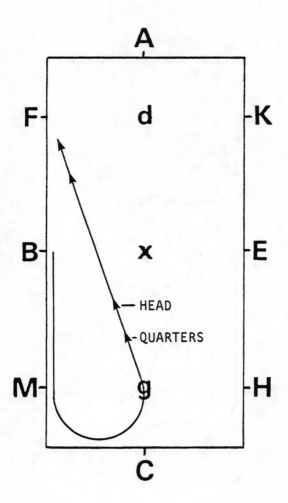

Fig 7   Correct

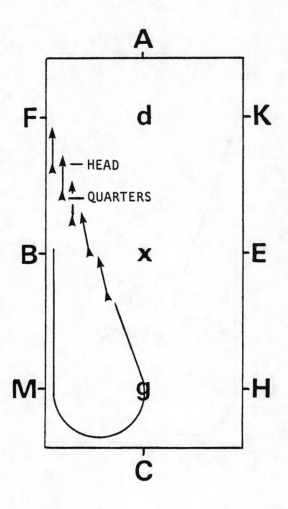

Fig 8   Incorrect

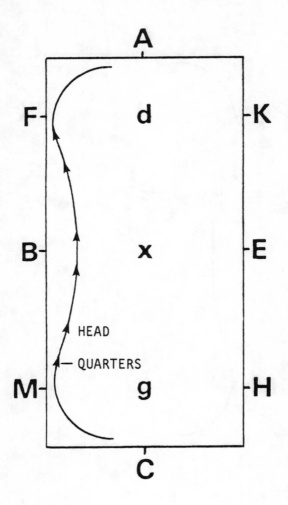

Fig 9   Correct

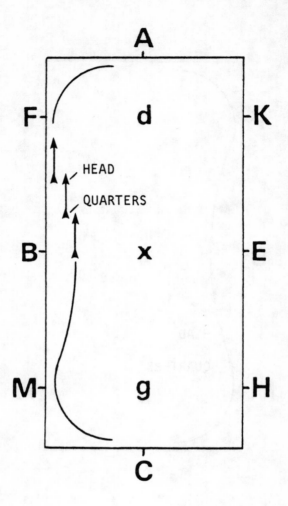

Fig 10   Incorrect

This is not the intention, it means that the rider has drawn in the front of the horse by hand aids which are too strong and not brought the hind quarters up under the horse in the correct manner, before taking hold of the front.

Correction

In all the horse's training the rider must consider the horse's mouth and the engagement of the hind quarters.

There must be no resistance in the mouth as this prevents the hindquarters from becoming engaged.

On the other hand the horse must be going forward in order to 'make the mouth'.

Therefore the two must develop together and the rider by the equal use of the hand and leg must bring the horse together. More pressure by the hands, not being supported by the legs can cause the appearance of the forehand or 'neck' being shortened, therefore the rider must work hard to equal the pressure of hand on the rein and leg on the horse's sides.

Obviously, for a moment one may be heavier than the other, but always aim at returning to the 'equal' amount of pressure.

NOT ACCEPTING HAND

This means that there is resistance in the mouth of the horse, when contact or extra contact is taken by the hand. It manifests itself in many ways, some of which are opening the mouth, tongue hanging out, coming above the bit, leaning on the bit, tossing the head, etc.

Correction

The correction must be in the acceptance of the bit, discussed on page 1.

However if the rider expects the horse to accept his hand aids, he must give the horse a contact which is reciprocal and this needs a good deal of understanding. A contact which never varies is not acceptable as it is a dead feel with no conversation for the horse to follow.

No contact is not acceptable either, as the horse then has no security, nor can he answer a light aid as the rein contact has to be 'taken up' by the rider and usually results in a jerk on the mouth.

The rider must aim to start with a firm but gentle contact with no slack in the rein, the variation coming from a slight closing or easing of the fingers, which is so slight as not to be seen by an onlooker. Much of the lightness of the hands is achieved by the rider having supple elbows and wrists, and good concentration.

NOT BETWEEN HAND AND LEG

Usually means that the horse is not sufficiently under control, as the rider's hand and leg aids are not co-ordinated. If the co-ordination is lacking then the horse can escape and instead of being brought together by the rider, his body left to his own devices will be inclined to wander.

Correction

Some riders are fortunate to have natural co-ordination and seldom have to think about it. Those who do not, have to work hard. They should aim to begin with, to have equal pressure leg to hand. In other words, never allow the hands to work stronger than the legs, and vice-versa. There are obviously going to be moments when there must be some alteration. This advice is only a basis to work on.

The hands and legs are there to 'talk' to the horse and constantly tell him what to do and where to go. If the contact of both are unsteady the conversation will be disjointed and the understanding not clear.

Therefore good co-ordination is vital to the horse's ability to obey his rider. Riders, please note!

NOT ENOUGH EXTENSION

This means that the horse is not showing enough length of stride.

Correction

The rider must bear in mind that in the various standard tests different degrees of extension are required, i.e. the extension in Elementary dressage tests is not so great as in Medium dressage tests, etc.

However, the basic requirements for extension are the same and only the amount asked for varies.

First. The horse must be capable of putting his hind legs in the right place so that he can carry himself without losing balance and rhythm.

Second. He must be able to cope with the necessary impulsion. The rider must not try to ask for the extension before he has achieved a degree of collection.

Only if the horse can collect himself properly will he then be in a position to extend, having the hind legs and the impulsion in the right place.

Many horses who do not show much promise in their lengthening at first, will eventually often show a good extension if the collection is improved. (For collection, see page 34).

NOT ENOUGH ANGLE (Shoulder in)

This comment is usually made in connection with the shoulder in movement, and means that the rider has not asked the forehand to come sufficiently off the track.

Correction

If the horse has been taught the shoulder in correctly then it is up to the rider to ask for the correct amount of angle. Sometimes it feels as though one has, and the judge disagrees. Therefore, it may be necessary to do a little more than you think is needed, for the judge.

However there are mistakes which as riders, we must not make.

First. It is easy to push the quarters 'out' rather than ride the forehand in off the track. Also, it is easy to get too much bend in the neck only, which is not a true shoulder in. The rider must remember that it is the whole front of the horse from the saddle forwards which must be positioned, and that the outside rein plays a bigger part than the inside rein in controlling this position.

Another failing, is to allow the outside shoulder to 'fall out', but here again, if the outside rein is used correctly, this should not happen.

When teaching shoulder in to the young horse, it may help to begin at walk to give the horse the idea of the aids.

Only when the horse can trot on short steps in preparation for collection can he be asked to shoulder in at trot, and then only for a short distance.

This is such a vital exercise which the rider uses all through the training to control or position the forehand, that it must be done correctly to be of value.

If the rider is doubtful how to begin shoulder in, here are some suggestions.

Begin in walk and start with a slight flexion to the inside hand to make sure that the horse will yield when the rein is taken. Position the forehand by riding the forelegs off the track after a corner so that the horse is already slightly curved.

When the forelegs are off the track, the hind legs must be kept on the track by the use of the rider's inside leg, and the horse asked to maintain impulsion and go sideways by the use of that leg.

The rider's outside leg will control the quarters and maintain the bend round the inside leg.

The outside rein will control the direction and the speed, also the amount of position. Usually an angle of not more than 45° is acceptable.

The point of the exercise is for the rider to have greater control of the forehand. If he is able to put the forehand where he wants to he will be able to position and prepare the horse much better for a variety of movements. Also he will be able to effect straightening of the horse at any time by correcting the front.

NOT ENOUGH DIFFERENCE

This term is generally used when an alteration within a pace is required, i.e. extension to collection, working to medium, etc. It means that the difference in the length of the stride is not sufficiently shown.

The transition from one requirement to the other was not 'marked', and took too long.

Correction

First the rider should try to ascertain by watching an expert, or having tuition on the various differences in the paces, so that he knows what is expected and how much extension or collection etc. he is aiming for.

He must know how to shorten the strides for collection, without restricting the horse, and how to lengthen the strides without allowing the hind legs to go out behind the horse, or letting him fall on his forehand.

He must know how much impulsion is needed and the differences in the outline of the horse.

Generally speaking, in collection, the horse appears more together and comes higher in front having his hind legs more under him, and in extension the head and neck are slightly stretched and the appearance of the horse is longer. Having discovered what the differences in the paces are, the rider must show by the transitions into and out of the pace variations, the difference between them.

In other words if going from a working pace to a medium pace, the rider must show at the required marker, a definite change from what he was doing previously.

From the medium to the working pace the horse must make the transition at the marker in a very few strides, not drift into it.

NOT ENOUGH FROM BEHIND
This term usually means that the hind legs are not doing their job sufficiently and are possibly taking rather a shallow step, not enough under the horse.

Correction

To develop more 'push' from the back legs, the rider must first put them in the right place. This means correcting the balance (see page 6).

Making the horse active and building up some impulsion (see page 29).

Once the energy is sufficiently 'stored' in the quarters, the horse should have plenty of power to push himself more forward.

NOT ENOUGH COLLECTION
This term is used when the collected paces are deficient in one way or another. That is to say: the hind legs are not engaged enough; the steps are too long; the forehand of the horse is too low.

It is also used when a particular exercise is asked for such as a canter pirouette. The judge not only has to look at the pirouette, but also to see if the horse was sufficiently collected during the movement.

Correction

True collection is one of the most difficult things to achieve and only a master of the art will probably do so.

However, the rest of us must try and there are some mistakes which some people make of which we must beware.

1. One of the most common is to draw the horse in from the front too much so that his neck is shortened and his nose in, but the body is not brought more together and the hind legs are not engaged.
2. Often the steps are shortened but the impulsion is lost so that eventually the horse shuffles.
3. The horse is brought back to a slower speed but the quarters are not asked to be active and the forehand is not raised.

I think therefore the rider must aim to slow the horse so that he can come into shorter steps and having done so, he must make sure that the hindlegs stay active, using the schooling whip, *not* harder leg aids. Do not ask for too much impulsion as the horse must find his own balance in these shorter steps and too much impulsion will create a problem for him.

The rider should only ask for a few steps at a time to start with and although he must 'sit', should not attempt to grind his seat into the saddle. Sit as quietly and as still as possible and let the horse find out how to manage himself.

The rider must use the half halts to help to achieve the shortening.

There must be no resistance to the hand and the horse must stay *straight*.

When the horse has learned to come into the shorter strides and if he is accepting the hand and staying straight, the impulsion may be built up.

Eventually the hind quarters must carry the main load of the horse and the forehand will come higher as the result of their greater ability and strength. All this takes quite a long time and cannot be hurried. The horse must be systematically schooled and his muscles developed by exercises so that there is no strain. (For comments on half halts, see page 4).

NOT FORWARD ENOUGH

This may be difficult to understand, but most judges mean that although the horse may be on the bit and in a nice rhythm, etc. he is not working with enough energy and because of this he is lacking in length of stride and not enough impulsion.

Correction

Without spoiling the balance and rhythm, or the head carriage, the rider must ask the horse to be more active (using the schooling whip) and build up a little more impulsion which will help to take the horse more forward.

Make sure that there is no resistance to the hand, as this could cause a block, which will prevent the horse from going forward enough. (For additional comments on the acceptance of the bit and impulsion, see pages 1 and 29).

NOT LOWERING ENOUGH

This usually applies to the walk on a long or free rein, and means that when the rider gives the rein, the horse instead of stretching his neck out and down, does the opposite.

Correction

If the horse does not naturally lower when the rein is eased and some do not, the rider should work to improve the horse's mouth (see page 1) which should work the neck muscles in such a way that when the rein is given the horse will stretch correctly.

The horse will also probably need suppling exercises such as shoulder in (see page 45) to stretch the stiff muscles which are holding him back when the rein is given.

NOT OVERTRACKING

In medium, extended and free walk, medium and extended trot, the imprint of the hind foot of the horse should come beyond the imprint left by the forefoot on the same side, i.e. the near hind should go beyond the near fore and the off hind beyond the off fore.

Correction

If the horse is not overtracking, he may possibly be restricted, i.e. held back by the rider and not able to take a good length of stride.

The rider must make certain that he is allowing the horse to move as naturally as possible, particularly in the walk. Where the stride should be the maximum length the horse will give with the rider keeping a light contact, but allowing the horse to move his head and neck up and down which he needs to do for his balance. Later in the training, the horse will need to be collected in the walk, but many are spoilt by doing this too soon.

In the trot, the rider must aim to have the horse relaxed, as stiff muscles often cause short strides to occur. With relaxation, good rhythm and balance, the horse should be able to bring his hind legs well forward and should then overtrack.

A few horses have a conformation which makes it very difficult or nearly impossible for them to overtrack, but usually some slight improvement can be made.

NOT ON CENTRE LINE

This comment is fairly obvious, but it is surprising how often one has to use it when judging and how difficult it seems to be for many horses and riders to remain straight on the centre line.

Correction

Sometimes there is a clearly defined line, sawdust, mown or painted.

If so the rider must follow this line and if he has taught

his horse to go straight, it should not be a terrible problem. At home, he must practice on a line making sure that the horse is accustomed to it and will not step aside as he meets it.

If he should 'wobble' off the line, the rider must return to it and not continue on a parallel line next to it, as this will lose even more marks.

If there is no defined line, the rider must aim at the 'C' marker, which helps in any case, and by keeping it in sight between the horse's ears so that he can be kept straight.

NOT STRAIGHT
This expression occurs many times in many different instances. It may refer to the head and neck, to the body, or the legs.

Correction
From the very first moment the rider sits on his horse, he must aim to achieve perfect straightness, in order that the horse will develop evenly on both sides, will take even steps and not become one sided. The rider must look at the horse's head and neck in front of him to keep the horse straight. Many people ride with the front bent round one way all the time. The rider must have an even contact. The horse's body must be kept straight between the rider's legs.

The hind legs must follow the track of the forelegs.

In particular the horse must be straight in all his transitions and the transition is not performed unless it is so.

This is one of the very important basic principles to which the rider must pay special attention, because much of the future training depends on this being correct.

NOT SQUARE
Refers to the halt and means that the four feet have not

stopped with a leg at each corner, so that the horse is balanced. The hind feet should be directly behind the fore feet, so that from the front, only the fore legs are seen.

Correction

Some horses will naturally come to a square halt, if they are balanced, but most horses will stop with one leg not in line with the other, usually a hind leg.

If the horse persistently leaves the same leg back, the rider should use his whip gently on that leg to move it up. Someone should be on the ground to see if the horse halts square or not and to tell the rider which leg is at fault, as it is not always easy to tell. The rider should try to concentrate on the movement of the legs in the last strides before the halt. That way he should be able to 'feel' which leg is doing what, and as a result, where they are at the halt. If the rider can develop this 'feel', then the halts should improve.

Also if there is no resistance in the mouth and the horse is kept up to the bridle with the legs, the halts should come square.

NOT TRACKING UP

This is when the hind legs of the horse are idle and they do not reach the imprint left by the fore leg which they should do, except in the collected paces.

Correction

There are two separate problems.

First, one may have a horse which is lazy and lacking impulsion and will not put itself out to take a good length stride. This horse must be 'woken up' with the use of the schooling whip so that he then has more energy to take him forward.

The second horse may be the complete opposite, but because he is headstrong, the rider has constantly to restrain him. Instead of taking long strides the horse will take short hurried steps always, seemingly, trying to keep up with himself.

This horse must first be slowed down and got into a relaxed condition by quiet slow work. Only when relaxed will he then begin to make longer steps which may take quite a while to obtain the required length. It does take a good deal of patience, and constant correction. The horse should also be allowed to lower his head and neck which will come with the relaxation and will also help to lengthen the strides. Half halts will help with this situation (see page 4).

OFF THE BIT
Maybe the horse has altered his head position for a moment due to a loss of balance, resistance to the aids, or the rein contact may be broken by the rider. Sometimes regretably the horse is never on the bit due to the ignorance of the rider who does not know how to obtain it.

Correction
The rider should first check up on the correct acceptance of the bit and make sure he knows what is right and knows what the possible evasions are.

Then he should correct the impulsion which may be lacking, allowing the horse to drop behind the bridle.

Next the rein contact must be steady and acceptable to the horse. Then it is up to the rider to concentrate and keep the horse between hand and leg. If his co-ordination is satisfactory the horse should not be able to come off the bit.

A momentary mistake in training is not a major disaster, but continuous mistakes can become a habit and should be avoided.

(For ACCEPTANCE OF THE BIT, see page 1).

ON THE FOREHAND

The weight of the horse instead of being evenly distributed over all four legs, comes more over the front legs causing the forehand of the horse to be lower than it should be, preventing the horse operating efficiently and easily.

Correction

The answer lies in the balance being improved and the rider being aware that due to the horse being naturally heavy in front, due to the position of the head and neck, the weight should gradually be transferred into the hindquarters. The use of the half halts and the gradual increase in the strength of the muscles in the hind quarters should be the chief method of transferring the weight.

Once the horse is strong enough and is able to put his hind legs sufficiently under the body, which is the result of systematic work, he should come light in front.

The horse cannot work easily if he is on the forehand. It is a hindrance not only to him, but also to his rider, who must be constantly pulled forwards with too much weight in his hands, not a comfortable situation, and one which is all too common. If the rider is not sure what exercises to practice to help this correction, apart from the half halts, he should try working in better balance and rhythm on circles mainly in trot and use the transitions from trot to walk and vice versa, making sure that the hind quarters are not lazy.

(For additional comments on half halts and balance, see pages 4 and 6).

ON THE HAND

This expression is used when the horse is allowed to lean on the bit using the rider's hands as support.

Correction

Check up on the horse's balance as he is probably taking too much weight on the forehand.

Use half halts to correct this. Do not allow the horse to gradually push down on the bit. At all times he must accept the bit. (For additional comments on the acceptance of the bit, half halts and balance, see pages 1, 4 and 6.

ON TWO TRACKS
Normally, when the horse is going forwards, the hind legs should follow the track of the forelegs, but sometimes the horse may swing his quarters over, lose his balance or mistake his rider's aids and instead of going straight forward, there will be some sideways movement as well. Then the horse is said to be, 'on two tracks'.

Correction

Really the rider must be more aware of the importance of the straightness of the horse and in making sure that the hindlegs do follow the forelegs, especially on circles and around corners.

At no time should the rider's legs allow the quarters to 'fall in', or 'fall out'.

Check up that the head and neck are straight and not too much bent. Very often there is more bend in the neck than in the rest of the horse. As the horse's spine does not permit him to do more than a slight curve, the neck should only do the same.

A neck bend will often make the quarters swing out. The rider then tries to correct this with the outside leg and the horse may swing the other way which will put him on two tracks.

OUTLINE NOT MAINTAINED
Some judges will use the expression outline, some silhouette, meaning the same thing.

When the outline or silhouette is not maintained, it means that the position of the horse's head and neck, the roundness of his back and the engagement of the quarters was correct at times, but did not stay the same throughout the test.

The outlines are different for the Novice horse compared to the Advanced horse, as the centre of balance is further back in the advanced horse.

Correction

The rider should try to find out from an 'expert', what the correct outline should be for his horse at the various stages of training.

Having done so he must endeavour to establish it, by working on the acceptance of the bit, the balance and the activity of the hind quarters. When these are under control and steady, the horse will be able to 'carry himself', without disturbance and his outline should stay the same.

OVERBENT

This is an expression used when the horse is bent too much at the poll and the nose is behind the vertical. The horse has the appearance of 'leading' with his forehand.

Correction

The horse becomes overbent for several reasons.

1. He may have too much impulsion and be 'racing' into the bridle. Too much pressure on the bit, caused by the rider trying to gain control, may make him draw his nose in too far, so it it is almost on his chest.

In this case, the first thing to do is to reduce impulsion by slowing the horse down to a controllable speed.

It will be necessary to use half halts as the pressure on the bit must vary. The rider may feel that he is going too slowly but this would be preferable to the horse being overstrong. Once a slower speed is established, the rider should endeavour to take a light contact and ride the horse in a normal manner.

2. Also the horse may become overbent due to a lack of impulsion. If the rider is not using his legs adequately asking the horse to go up into the bridle, the horse may well hang behind the bit with his head overbent at the poll. In this case the rider must maintain the contact with the bit, but increase the activity of the hind legs to create some more impulsion. This should take the horse forward enough to make him raise his head to the correct position.

However, if the horse gets into the habit of being overbent, he may like the idea and however hard the rider tries to make the corrections, the horse may not want to come into the right position. In this case, the rider may have to 'lift' the horse's head and neck by raising one or both hands for a brief moment until it comes into a better position. This may have to be repeated several times to achieve the correction.

3. The horse may have been over-bitted or restricted by the rider's hands, but as long as the rider ensures that the bit is acceptable and so are his hands, then the foregoing corrections may be applied.

A correction will not be achieved by loosening the rein contact. (For comments on HALF HALTS, see page 4).

OVER THE BIT
This is similar to being overbent and usually means that the horse is on the forehand, or leaning on the hand, or possibly all three. In any case the weight of the horse is too much on the front and is not accepting the bit lightly with his head in the correct position.

Correction

See **OVERBENT**, page 57.

OVERTRACKING See **NOT OVERTRACKING**, page 50.

PACE NOT TRUE

This means that the pace which is criticised is not in the correct time, i.e. walk should be four time, trot two and canter three time.

It is possible for the horse to move his legs like a 'pacer', both legs on the same side coming forward together. This could occur in walk or trot.

In canter, it is possible for the horse to canter in four time instead of three, each hoof coming to the ground at a different time.

There could also be too much suspension in the trot pace making it more like a passage than trot. This comment might be used in any of these instances.

Correction

The paces sometimes go wrong due to tenseness of the horse, mentally or physically. Therefore it may be a good idea to make sure that the horse is relaxed and not too keyed up.

Too much or too little impulsion may also cause problems.

The rider must try to assess whether he is working the horse with the correct amount.

Resistance in the mouth can also cause the paces to become incorrect. Therefore the rider must also check that the horse is accepting the bit.

If the trot is too high and too much like passage, the impulsion must be directed more forwards and the tempo of the steps quickened by increasing the speed slightly.

(For comments on **ACCEPTANCE OF THE BIT**, see page 1).

PIVOTED

This refers to the hind legs of the horse in a pirouette in walk. In a correct pirouette, the hind legs should remain mobile and should march up and down on the spot. If one of the legs 'sticks' and is not picked up, the horse may be said to have pivoted.

Correction

When teaching the horse the pirouette the rider must first be able to 'collect' the walk a little, so that the steps are short and bouncy.

The quarters must be well under control and when the turn is commenced there must be no swinging into the rider's outside leg. In fact as the rider takes the forehand sideways and round, the horse must, if anything, step away from the outside leg of the rider.

At first the turn must be performed quite large so that the hind legs do keep on the move and the turn should be done slowly step by step, so that control can be maintained.

POSITIONING INSUFFICIENT

This means that the rider has failed to prepare the horse for a movement, i.e. by putting him into a position where he will be able to perform the exercise easily.

Correction

Riders are not always fully aware of the difficulties the horse encounters if he is not in balance, or if his rider requires him to do something with too little warning.

Positioning mainly refers to the forehand and the control the rider has, or does not have, over it. The rider should be able to use the shoulder in exercise to aid his control of the shoulders and the forehand and if he is going to ride a corner or a circle he will use the shoulder in position in a very minor degree to prepare the horse.

In this way the shoulders do not fall out and the horse is more under control and better balanced.

Similarly, in the canter it may be necessary to use a shoulder in position to a minor degree to straighten the canter, if the quarters show signs of 'falling in'. (For comments on the SHOULDER IN, see page 45).

PREPARATION INSUFFICIENT

This means that the rider has not warned the horse early enough what is coming next and was probably unbalanced which may cause many other things to go wrong.

Correction

Riders must know what they are about to do, and at what pace. This may sound obvious, but many riders do not determine in their own minds exactly what they want to do, so that they can prepare the horse.

The route and pace having been decided, the rider must warn the horse by some preparatory aids. If he is going forward, he should slightly increase the pressure of the aids for a second to gain the horse's attention.

If he wishes to slow down it may be necessary to use the half halts to ensure that the balance is correct before trying the next exercise. Particularly applicable in regard to all transitions if they are to be accurate at the markers.

Riders please note, that if the horse has his head in the air, is crooked, or has too much or too little energy, he will not be able to do anything satisfactorily. These things must be put right before any attempt can be made to proceed to the next movement.

QUARTERS IN OR OUT

'Quarters out' means that instead of the hind legs following the forelegs which they should do, they are on a track to the outside of the forelegs. 'Quarters in' means the opposite, the hind legs are on an inner track to the forelegs.

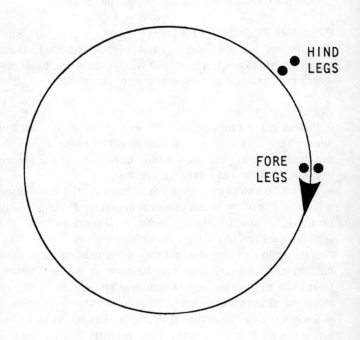

Labels in figure:
- HIND LEGS
- FORE LEGS

Fig 11   Quarters out

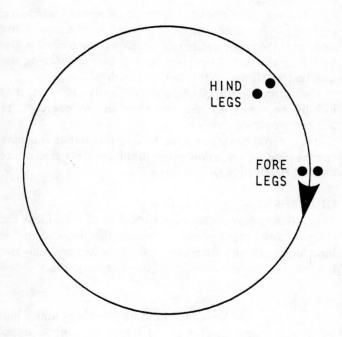

HIND
LEGS

FORE
LEGS

Fig 12 Quarters in

Correction

In the case of the quarters falling out, the rider must first check that he is able to ride the horse on a straight line with the hindlegs following the forelegs. Then he must achieve a correct bend with the hindlegs still following the forelegs.

Only a very slight bend at first and using the outside leg against the horse to control any possible evasion. If the rider uses too much inside rein or allows more bend in the neck than the rest of his horse he will be encouraging the quarters to fall out, so this must be avoided.

The correction for quarters in is slightly different, it is usually necessary to use the shoulder in exercise, to achieve the straightening.

It is a mistake to try to push the quarters out as this may cause swinging and many other problems. (For comments on the SHOULDER IN, see page 45).

QUARTERS NOT ENGAGED

This problem may not be easy to feel or to see unless the rider is fairly experienced. It means that instead of the hind legs working under the horse, they are probably out behind, and there is insufficient bend of the joints.

Correction

The horse must be made to put his hind legs under him by first putting him at a speed where he cannot propel himself forward without bringing the hind legs under the body. This speed is usually quite slow and should be arrived at by the use of half halts which will improve the balance so that the horse will carry himself.

Once the hind legs come in the right place the joints will automatically bend more and if asked for more activity by the use of the schooling whip, the quarters will then be doing their job effectively.

If the quarters are to be physically developed to their maximum strength, which they need to be to carry the horse through to advanced standard, the hind legs must be put in the right place from the start so that the horse may learn to carry himself in balance. (For comments on HALF HALTS, see page 4).

QUARTERS LEADING OR TRAILING

1. The comment is in connection with the half pass in which the horse should travel forwards and sideways, with his body although bent in the direction he is going, remaining parallel to the side of the arena.

2. On some occasions the quarters may be over too far, ahead of the forehand.

3. In other instances the quarters will hardly be over at all and the horse is not crossing his hind legs.

Correction

To teach the horse the half pass, the rider must first make sure he can take a flexion of the head and neck to one side or the other, keeping the remainder of the horse straight.

He must be able to come up the centre line with this flexion and when this is easy he should draw his outside leg back, taking the forehand over with his rein aids and controlling the quarters, ask them over as well. He must feel whether there is too much 'swing over' of the quarters to his leg, and he must feel whether there is enough reaction to his leg and if not, use the schooling whip to assist the leg.

When the horse will go sideways slowly under control, the rider may glance over his shoulder briefly to see where the quarters are, or if he has a friend on the ground he can

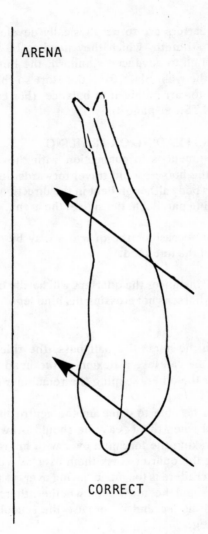

Fig 13   Left Half pass — correct

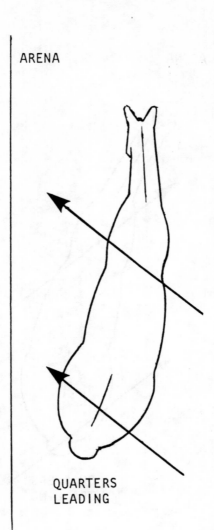

ARENA

QUARTERS
LEADING

Fig 14 Left half Pass — quarters leading

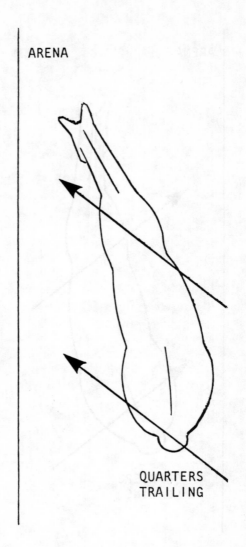

ARENA

QUARTERS
TRAILING

Fig 15   Left half pass — quarters trailing

obtain his help until he can feel what is happening for himself.

It is usually wise to begin in walk until the horse has understood the aids.

QUARTERS SWINGING
This means that the hind quarters are not under control between the rider's legs.

Correction

During the horse's training he must be taught to accept a light even pressure from the rider's legs without taking his quarters from side to side in evasion. The rider must make sure that his horse does accept the legs and will go forward straight, from light aids. Even though the horse may dislike the feel of the legs against his sides, he will accept thim in time, if the rider quietly persists.

Sometimes the quarters may get out of control due to having too much impulsion which cannot easily be controlled or because there is loss of balance.

The horse's quarters could also swing due to resistance in the mouth. The rider must first ascertain what the problem is and then carefully work on correcting it.

QUICKENED RATHER THAN EXTENDED
This comment ties in with 'RUNNING AND RUSHING' (see page 72). It means that instead of the horse taking a longer stride in the same rhythm he probably goes onto the forehand and hurries along at a faster speed.

Correction

When teaching the horse to become extended, the rider should first teach some collection to properly engage the hind quarters. If they are under the horse and active, he will be able to 'push' himself off into a longer stride which should have some elevation. The rider must allow the energy he has built up by shortening or collecting the stride, to go forward but not 'down in front'. He must keep the balance level and although not allowing the horse to 'lean', he must expect rather a stronger contact due to increased impulsion.

Do not expect too much at first. The horse must gradually build up to his extension over a period of time. If too much is asked at first, the balance and rhythm will be lost.

The horse should 'offer' to go on a longer stride due to the increase of energy in the quarters caused by the collection. The rider should take what is offered to begin with. Later, it may be necessary to tap the horse with the schooling whip to make him give more. (For comments on COLLECTION, see pages 34 and 48).

REGULAR

Refers to the even-ness with which the horse puts his feet to the ground. Each step must be at a regular speed, rhythm and an even length. There must be no break in the regularity of the steps.

Correction

To achieve regularity, the balance of the horse must be as perfect as possible and he must be without resistance. (For comments on the ACCEPTANCE OF THE BIT and BALANCE, see pages 1 and 6).

REIN BACK CROOKED

In the rein back, the steps should be even and straight and in two time. One pair of diagonal legs and then the other.

When it is crooked, the quarters usually swing one way or the other and the strides will be uneven and possibly not in two time either.

Correction

First, check on the mouth and the acceptance of the bit,

if there is resistance to the hand, the quarters will inevitably swing.

When using the rein aids, the rider should aim at one step at a time, increasing the pressure on the mouth and then easing immediately the horse steps back.

If the horse puts his head in the air, or hollows his back, on no account attempt to rein back as it is almost physically impossible. Make sure he goes back evenly between the rider's leg aids which should be light and even. Too much 'pushing' by the legs will hinder the horse and confuse him as he will think he is meant to go forward.

The rider may lean very slightly forward to allow the horse to use his back, which will come rounder as he steps back.

Concentrate on the straightness and ease of the movement.

(For comments on ACCEPTANCE OF THE BIT, see page 1).

RESTING LEG
Applies to the halt where the horse should be taking an even weight on all four legs. In this instance he may be resting one leg and only standing on three.

Correction
The rider must bring the horse to the halt in a balanced manner so that the weight is evenly distributed.

However, a fault which does allow this to happen is if the rider takes his legs away from the horse at the halt which makes him feel unsupported and gives him the opportunity to rest a leg.

Also, during training the rider must ensure that the hocks are coming under the horse in the halt, and that they are not left behind.

If the quarters are not engaged, it will be more difficult to keep the legs under control.

RESTRICTED

Means that the rider has for one reason or another held the pace back so that it is too slow, or he may cause the stride to be too short so that the horse cannot use himself.

Correction

Restriction often occurs because the horse is pulling or trying to go too fast and the rider tries to keep him under control with the hands only. Usually the horse will become slower without excessively engaging the hind quarters. He may become overbent and shorten his stride so that he hardly puts one foot in front of the other.

The rider must endeavour to gain control over the speed by using half halts and when the horse is better balanced and going on a lighter rein, he will then be more relaxed. With the relaxation comes a longer stride. The rider must then concentrate on the rhythm and keeping the horse light on the hand.

RUNNING

This term is usually used when the horse is dashing along too fast on the forehand, with no balance or rhythm and very little suspension in the stride.

Correction

See 'RUSHING', page 72.

RUSHING

This generally means that the pace is too hurried and that there is a lack of balance and rhythm.

Correction

The rider is in control of the paces, or should be, and it is up to him to know when his horse is balanced and to keep the pace steady.

Some horses are more impetuous than others and do want to surge forwards or keep increasing the speed. The rider must use the half halts to achieve greater control over the paces and if the horse learns to carry himself in balance he will find it much easier not to rush.

If constantly reminded in the beginning, horses will learn to go at a particular speed at each pace and will not expect to go faster all the time. The rider is responsible for teaching this to the horse.

In no way must the rider hang on to the horse's head to slow him down. This may cause the horse to pull against the rider. If the half halts are used correctly this should not happen.

The rider must always be aware of the rhythm of the footfalls in the various paces so that he can regulate the strides. (For additional comments on HALF HALTS and BALANCE, see pages 4 and 6).

RESISTING

Refers to any desire from the horse to evade his rider's aids. For example, he may open his mouth, cross his jaw, put his tongue out, tilt his head, swing his quarters, kick to the leg or just plain 'nap'.

Correction

If the evasion is in the mouth the improvement must be made by correcting the acceptance of the bit. Once the horse is 'giving' in his jaw the rider should be able to overcome the resistance.

If the horse is evading the leg aids, the rider must first pay attention to whether the horse is going forwards willingly to a light aid. If not, he must use the schooling whip, to assist the leg. If necessary the whip may have to be applied quite firmly at first, until the horse respects it and will then go forward from a light tap.

If he kicks to the leg, the stick should be used immediately after each kick until it stops. Many riders do not follow this through thinking that the more they use the stick the more the horse kicks. However, if this resistance is to be overcome, the rider must persist with the stick until the horse will accept the feel of it being applied.

'Napping' of course can be a great problem especially if allowed to become confirmed.

The rider should be very careful to not allow the young horse to find out his own strength. He should be guided firmly but with care to the rider's wishes, which if explained properly should cause no problem. However, mistakes are made and if the same mistake is made too often the horse will soon take advantage.

It is a mistake to think that one cannot be really firm with the young horse. He must know that when the rider wishes to go forward, he must go, and when asked to accept the bit he must do so. This should be the rider's first job. It should not be left as it so often is, with the horse being ridden on a loose rein for several months. He then learns to go that way and when the rider takes a contact he usually objects.

With the older horse which is spoilt, it is much more complicated to overcome nappiness or resistance and expert help may be needed. The best advice I can give, is to go back to the beginning and start again! Treat the horse as a youngster and go through the basic programme making the correction as and when required.

The rider must bear in mind that if a horse has been ridden incorrectly for years, all his muscles and his physique may be developed incorrectly and it will take great patience and much riding of the school exercises to soften the hard muscles, so that the horse is able to change his way of going.

He may not be resisting because he is a 'pig' but simply because he has been badly ridden and the rider will have to use all his intelligence and knowledge on the correct basic training to enable the changes to take place. (For comments on the ACCEPTANCE OF BIT, see page 1).

ROUGH TRANSITION
See TRANSITION ROUGH, Page 86.

SHOULDERS FALLING OUT
Indicates that the rider has lost control of the forehand and is allowing the shoulders of the horse to be breaking the true line of the curve, or the straight line.

Correction

The rider must be well aware of the use of his outside rein and leg when riding a curve.

He must avoid too much bend of the neck which will give a false curve and allow the shoulders to fall out.

He should ask for the bend with the inside rein and leg, but then control the amount with the outside rein and leg. He should aim at being able to ride a curve with the outside rein and inside leg, with a *very* light inside rein contact.

He must make sure that the horse is not deviating from the correct line of the curve as shown.

STIFF
This comment occurs so often and means that whereas the horse should curve round a circle or a corner, he moves without bend or even flexion.

Correction

The horse to move efficiently must become supple in his back and must curve his whole length when on a circle or part of a circle, a corner etc.

First the rider must see whether he can produce a small head flexion to one side and then the other. The rider should feel one side of the mouth and turn the horse's

75

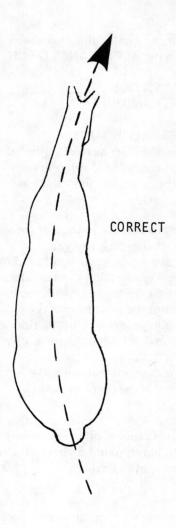

CORRECT

Fig 16   Riding curve or circle — correct

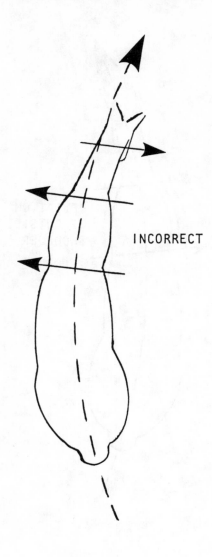

INCORRECT

Fig 17   Riding curve or circle — incorrect

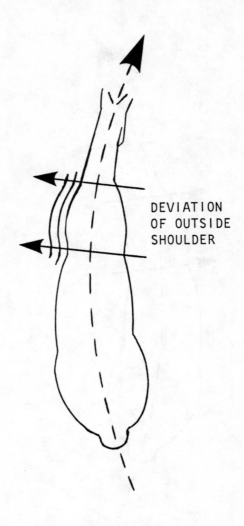

DEVIATION
OF OUTSIDE
SHOULDER

Fig 18   Deviation of outside shoulder

head very slightly to the same side. If the horse yields to the hand, then the rider may try the other side.

If all is well and the horse is even in his mouth, the rider should use the rein to achieve the flexion and then his leg to make some 'give' under the saddle. If the horse is 'dead' to the leg, use the schooling whip to achieve the result. When the leg is applied the horse must offer to move away from it. Then the outside rein and leg must 'catch' him and control the bend and make sure he is keeping to the line of the circle, etc.

Subsequently, the shoulder in exercise must be taught to increase the control of the forehand and make the muscles more supple by the increased bend and activity of the inside hind leg. (For comments on SHOULDER IN, see page 45).

STRIKE OFF LATE OR EARLY
Means that the canter did not start at the marker.

Correction

In training the rider will start his young horse, or an older horse who may not want to be obedient, on a corner, to help him strike off on the correct leg.

When this is understood by the horse, the rider must begin to make the strike off in other places and then finally at a precise point. He must make the horse very obedient to the lighest of aids so that with only a minimum of preparation he can ask for complete obedience and get the strike off where he wants it.

The schooling whip may have to be employed to achieve the obedience, but once the horse understands it, can be dispensed with.

SWISHING TAIL
Some horses will swish their tails during a test in an angry and resistant fashion.

Some may swing the tail occasionally for a moment.

In any case it may be classed as resistance and marked down in the submission.

Correction

Most horses swish their tails because there is some difficulty for them in a certain movement.

If they are trained correctly, with careful preparation and proper relaxation, the difficulties should not occur. With systematic physical development there will not be any reason to resist by tail swishing.

The horse must accept the rider's aids, particularly the legs. If there is hesitation it is preferable to use the schooling whip to overcome it at the start, then to wait and have trouble later.

In the case of the older horse, the problem will be difficult to stamp out, but the rider should pay attention to correcting the acceptance of the leg aids.

When the horse is using his back correctly, the tail will 'swing' from side to side in rhythm with the strides and will show no sign of stiffness in the dock.

Some tail swishing may be due to stiffness in the back and if the horse is made more supple it may then cease.

A suppling exercise which may help is the SHOULDER IN, (see page 45).

SWUNG ROUND

Is a comment made during a pirouette in walk or canter, when the horse has possibly turned on the centre, or made the turn too fast and not under control.

In the case of the canter pirouette the strides of the canter may be lost and the horse will swing or pivot on one or both hind legs.

Correction

Control over the stride is the important factor. The

horse must not be allowed to go at his own speed but to come round stride by stride. The strides must be of even size.

In the walk the four time pace must be maintained and when teaching the turn, the horse should be asked to go one step and then halt, until he has completed the turn. The rider can then control the steps and prevent the horse walking forwards or backwards. Also he can make sure that the quarters do not swing into the outside leg. He must lead the forehand round with his reins used equally, (not more pressure on the inside) easing the hand between each step. There should be a slight flexion to the way he is turning.

As soon as the horse understands the aids he must be asked to do the turn in walk and the hind legs will be expected to be mobile. Rather like marching on the spot. First, a semi-collected walk must be arrived at in order that the horse can turn almost on the same place. Later when the horse is in real collection the turn most be completely on the spot.

In canter the sequence of the steps (see page 19) must be maintained. The horse must canter in the turn, not rear round or fling himself sideways.

First a very collected canter must be achieved so that the horse can remain in balance almost on the spot, on the straight line.

Then he must give a bend to the way he will turn, only when these things are correct can the rider ask for the turn. The aids being the same as for the walk turn, with the inside leg maintaining the canter.

Usually in the half turn, four strides are asked for, and in a full turn, eight. The same number of strides should be shown in the left pirouette as in the right.

TENSE
Describes the state of the horse mentally and physically,

when he is 'worked up' either by outside distractions, or because he has not been taught to be relaxed.

Correction

It is necessary for the horse to be calm mentally if he is to be able to learn and remember what he is being taught.

He will be receptive only when he is unbothered in the mind and physically relaxed. Stiff, tense muscles cannot comply easily to the rider's aids.

How does one achieve this especially when some horses are much more lively than others.

Speed is one bugbear in the case of the tense horse. Usually he is too impulsive, so it is necessary to remove this by going very slowly, until the horse realises there is nothing to be excited about. Work on a large circle, in a steady trot, using half halts generally helps the horse to become quieter and less tense.

It may take longer to calm the canter, but work on the trot will eventually improve the whole situation. (For comments on HALF HALTS, see page 4).

TIPPING OR TILTING HEAD

Means that the face of the horse is not held vertically.

From the front the head is slanted to the right or to the left.

Correction

If the rider has trained his horse to go straight from the beginning, this problem should not occur. However mistakes are made and sometimes some tilting will occur, very often when the rider is trying to achieve a bend in half pass for instance.

To correct this condition it will be necessary to go back to the beginning, and try to obtain the straightness, paying great attention to the head and neck, and the evenness of the acceptance of the hands.

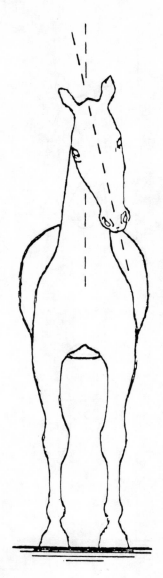

Fig 19   Head tilted

83

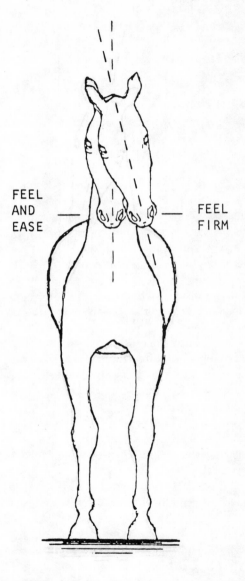

FEEL
AND
EASE

FEEL
FIRM

Fig 20   Correcting tilted head

If there is difficulty the rider may keep the feel firm on the side to which the nose is tilting, then feel and ease the hand on the other side to encourage the head to come straight.

TRIPPED
This means that during a movement the horse tripped in one or more strides.

Correction

Tripping is usually due to lack of, or loss of balance. This is usually the main cause.

Marks will be lost for persistent tripping as it shows lack of balance, but if it is only a momentary mistake in the case of a young horse, the judge will probably be quite lenient, so long as it does not affect the movement too much.

Some horses trip when they are fatigued, or if young, because they cannot organise their weight and that of their riders, very well.

The rider must make it as easy as possible for the horse to carry himself and his rider be sitting as still as possible and preventing the horse getting onto the forehand.

The horse's feet should be checked, as excessively long toes can cause tripping.

TRANSITION NOT DEFINED
The transitions as stated previously must be done at the designated marker.

Sometimes it is required that there should be a change of pace from medium to collected canter. This change of pace is also a transition and as such should show a distinct difference.

If the horse is allowed to 'drift' from one pace to the other the transition will hardly be seen and may be described as not defined.

Correction
See **NOT ENOUGH DIFFERENCE**, page 47.

TRANSITION ROUGH

During a test there are many transitions, or changes from one pace to another. These should be smooth, straight and balanced. Any resistance to the hand will make a transition rough.

Correction

The rider should know exactly where he wants to make a transition, so that he can 'prepare' the horse sufficiently.

The horse must be straight and not going too fast or he will be uncontrolled.

He must be in balance and the rider may use the half halts to achieve this state.

The rider must prepare the horse by a couple of 'warning' aids to make sure he is attentive, and then as the horse's head arrives at the marker he should ask for the transition, which should happen by the time the rider's leg reaches the marker smoothly and with no alteration of the head position.

The canter to trot transition always causes difficulty at first as the weight of the horse often falls forward and the rider will tip up onto the shoulders.

The rider must endeavour to balance the canter and shorten the strides before the transition. As soon as the horse breaks, the rider must sit up as steady as possible and immediately correct the trot speed which will have surged forward.

Once the horse has learned that he may not race forwards in trot he will gradually steady himself in the trot so long as the preparation in canter has been attended to. If there is lack of acceptance of the hand the horse will probably throw his head up or down which will also make the transition rough, so the rider should make sure that the horse will 'give' to the bit when extra contact is taken. (For additional comments on the ACCEPTANCE OF THE BIT and HALF HALTS, see pages 1 and 4).

TONGUE OUT
Sometimes the horse will put his tongue out of the side of his mouth. It may be for a moment, or he may do it continuously.

Either way it is an evasion of the bit.

Because the horse is not accepting the correct influence of the bit he will be severely penalised.

Correction

The rider should first make sure that there is nothing wrong with the bit, i.e. too sever, worn, pinching, etc.

Second, he should ensure that his hands are not causing the horse discomfort by having a too strong and unsympathetic contact. If these points seem alright he should try to work on the acceptance of the bit.

It may be worth having the teeth checked in case they are sharp. (For comments on the ACCEPTANCE OF BIT, see page 1).

TONGUE OVER THE BIT
This is an evasion, whereby the horse puts his tongue over the top of the bit instead of keeping it underneath thus getting away from the correct influence of the bit.

Correction

As the influence of the bit is lost if the tongue is put over it, the rider must do all he can to prevent this habit occurring in the first place.

Young horses sometimes develop the habit as the result of being left in the stable tacked up. They start to play around with the bit which is still strange to them and discover that it is more comfortable or more entertaining to alter the tongue position. Therefore it may be unwise to put the horse in this situation.

In the case of the older horse he may merely have discovered that he can be less easily controlled by putting the tongue over the mouthpiece. Therefore will do this whenever he wishes to evade the aids. The rider must try to achieve better acceptance of the bit, and employ the use of correctly fitted drop noseband to prevent the horse opening his mouth. (For comments on the ACCEPTANCE OF THE BIT, see page 1).

TOO LOW
Is really the same as being on the forehand and means that the whole front of the horse is carrying too much weight.

Correction
  See ON THE FOREHAND, page 55.

TURN ON CENTRE
Applies to a pirouette when the horse has failed to keep the hind quarters on the spot. The rider allows the horse to swing the quarters against the outside leg instead of keeping them still.

Correction
  See SWUNG ROUND, page 80.

UNBALANCED
This remark describes the state of the horse when he has lost his balance temporarily or completely.

If the balance is alright in the first place and the horse becomes unbalanced for a moment, he will probably be able to regain it again quite soon, and so will not lose many marks.

If however, the balance was not very good in the first place, the horse may find such difficulty in trying to perform several movements, that he may get on the forehand so much that the rider will be unable to regain control.

Some horses will go through the whole test in an unbalanced manner. Many marks will be forfeited in this case.

Correction

The rider must learn about balance, as it is up to him to put the weight in the right place. Some horses are naturally well balanced and others are not, but whatever the situation is, the rider must help the horse by distributing the weight evenly. (For comments on BALANCE, see page 6).

UNLEVEL

This is a reference to the strides of the horse and may be seen in walk and particularly in trot.

It means, for example, that instead of the front feet taking even weight as they come to the ground, one may be taking more than the other, giving the appearance of slight lameness.

The strides may also be uneven, one leg coming further forward than the other.

All this also applies to the hind legs and in addition one hock may come higher than the other.

Correction

Unlevelness can be caused in several ways. First, any unevenness in the acceptance of the bit can cause the horse to be unlevel or 'bridle lame'.

Secondly, if the physical development of the horse is uneven it will cause one-sidedness.

Most horses have a hollow side and a stiff side and the rider has to try to stretch the muscles on the hollow side and shorten the muscles on the stiff side to even them up.

He does this by using the school movements, circles, serpentines etc. and suppling exercises such as shoulder in.

It is important to ride straight lines as well as circles to make sure that the horse is working evenly. Should the muscles on one side be stronger than the other the horse will find it easier to push off harder with the strong hind leg. The weaker one may lag behind which will make the horse unlevel.

Riding on one diagonal only can cause uneven steps, so it is important to change the diagonal when changing the rein.

Riders must not expect drastic changes to take place. The horse will only even up over a period of time with patient and systematic work.

UNSTEADY HALT

This comment is used when the horse comes to the halt but does not really achieve immobility. He may fidget with his legs, or his head, or move off the line.

Correction
See MOVED AT HALT, page 38.

UNSTEADY HEAD

This remark describes the lack of steadiness of the head carriage.

Some horses may be unsteady in their head carriage throughout the test.

Some may be unsteady for a moment due to a loss of balance in the difficulty of a movement.

Correction
A steady head carriage is only achieved by good balance and the correct acceptance of the bit (see page 1). Balance must be maintained by the rider if the horse is to be able to

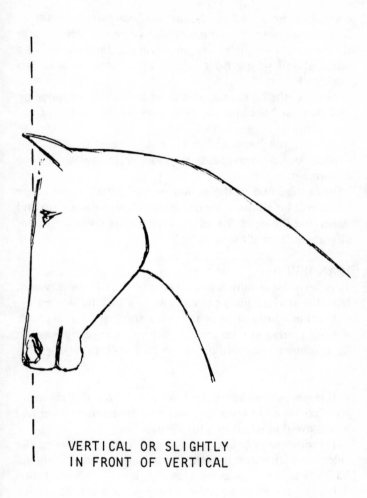

VERTICAL OR SLIGHTLY
IN FRONT OF VERTICAL

Fig 21   Head still — nose vertical

91

control his neck and head, which he will use naturally to balance himself. By being at the correct speed and in rhythm, any movement the horse will need to make will be minimal and so the rider is able to ask him to keep his head still.

In walk, the head and neck must be allowed to move up and down a little, this is necessary to the action of the walk strides.

In trot, the head and neck are more still and there should be a consistent position with relatively no movement.

In canter, due to the action of the canter strides, the horse will be allowed some movement of the neck up and down, but the head should be still with the nose vertical or slightly in front of the vertical.

WANDERING

This term is usually used when the horse has deviated from the straight line or circle, etc. on which he started.

In other words, if he is following the line of a 20 metre (66 feet) circle and he makes the circle larger or smaller for a moment, he could be said to be wandering.

Correction

If the horse 'wanders' it is usually the fault of the rider who has failed to keep him between the hand and leg and has allowed him to come 'off the aids'.

If the horse is being made to go forwards between the rider's leg aids and is kept at a steady speed, he should have enough energy going forwards into the bridle. If this is so, the rider will be able to keep a good contact with a steady rein between which the horse can go forward and straight. The horse should then be purposeful in his strides.

If the rider is decisive in his directions the horse will be clear in his mind and will be less likely to wander about.

WRONG BEND

Many riders fail to achieve the correct bend of the horse in the corners, circles etc. The horse should be slightly curved in the direction he is going. If this is incorrect many marks will be lost not only for wrong bend, but the resulting problems also, such as lack of balance, rhythm, etc.

Correction

The rider should first make sure that he can ride straight with even acceptance of the bit and leg aids.

Then he should try to make the horse flex to one hand and then the other. This should be very slight and is only done to check on the 'give' of each side of the mouth.

The horse must then also yield to the leg when it is applied. The schooling whip can be used to achieve this.

Once the horse will give to the hand and leg, a bend can be arrived at. The horse must be bent uniformly from nose to tail, with no more bend in the neck than the rest of the horse.

As the horse cannot physically bend his spine very much the bend is quite slight.

The rider must be able to change the bend from one rein to the other, but as the horse needs time to organise himself, the rider must prepare for the change of bend by riding straight for a few strides. The horse must accept a small flexion to the new direction on the straight before he is allowed to go round on the new rein.

Consideration must also be given to the outside leg of the rider which has to control the quarters and keep the bend round the inside leg. A true bend will not be achieved without this acceptance.

WRONG LEG NOT CORRECTED

This comment is used when the rider has allowed the horse to strike off in the canter with the wrong leg leading and does not put it right before the movement finishes. In this case the judge will very likely give no marks for that movement.

Correction

When cantering normally round the arena, the horse should lead with the inside foreleg, followed by the inside hind leg, and he should be bent in the direction he is going.

With the young or difficult horse, it will be as well to start on a corner with the horse straight, no flexion to either hand particularly. He may need to lengthen the trot strides a little at first, but soon he must answer the leg aids which can be backed up by the schooling whip held in the outside hand.

If there is any deviation from the track to the outside, the horse will almost certainly strike off wrong. In other words, if wishing to strike off to the right, the rider should feel that the balance is a little to the right, but definitely not in any way to the left. He must control the horse with his outside rein and leg. He may use the schooling whip against the outside shoulder if the horse persists in trying to go towards the outside of the track.

Too much bend in the neck will hinder the horse and this should be avoided.

The rider must learn to 'feel' which foreleg is coming forward in the strike off so that he knows before the canter really starts which leg the horse will be on. If the horse fails to make the correct strike off the rider must quickly bring him back to trot, check the balance and try again.